GIRAFFES OF BOTSWANA

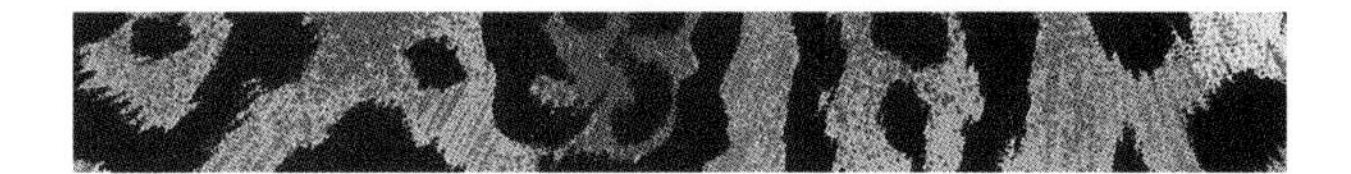

Written by Eduard Zingg

Published by Abdo & Daughters, 6535 Cecilia Circle, Edina, Minnesota 55439

Edited By: Jim Abdo and Bob Italia for Abdo & Daughters Publishing

Text and Photographs: Eduard Zingg
Illustrations and Maps: W. Michel and K. Wozniak

Library of Congress Cataloging-in-Publication Data

Zingg, Eduard, 1940-
Giraffes of Botswana / written by Eduard Zingg.
p. cm.
Includes index.
Summary: Introduces animals found in Botswana including the warthog, the giraffe, vervet monkey and leopard.
ISBN 1-56239-215-8
1. Giraffes -- Botswana -- Juvenile literature. 2. Mammals -- Botswana -- Juvenile literature. 3. Animal communities -- Botswana -- Juvenile literature. [1. Zoology -- Botswana. 2. Botswana.] I. Title.
QL737.U56Z56 1993
599. 73 '57 -- dc20 93-10265
CIP
AC

Table of Contents

WARTHOGS

While other animals have an air of nobility, warthogs have more homely characteristics. They are peaceful, busy little animals. They have hairless gray skin except for short bristles on the back. They have big warts below their eyes. That is how they get their name. Warthogs are 2 feet (.6 meters) long and stand 30 inches (76 centimeters) high at the shoulder. They weigh an average of 220 pounds (100 kilograms). The tusks are long, and curved upwards and sideways. They use their upper tusks for digging.

The lower tusks are used in fighting and for protection. When fleeing from its enemies, such as leopards, wild dogs, and cheetahs, the warthog follows a zig-zag course. It runs at full speed for its home, usually an abandoned antbear hill. At the last moment, it reverses into its home, to keep the tusks facing outward, protecting itself.

The warthog lives in the light forest or open bush. They stay close to water. It lives in small family groups. They like to wallow in mud baths. They feed on grass, roots and wild fruit.

When frightened, the warthog grunts loudly. Though normally peaceful, it fights back when attacked. Wild dogs have a respect for its tusks. Warthogs keep to themselves.

The warthog inhabits light forest or open bush, never far from water and is usually seen in small family groups.

Porcupines are the longest-lived rodents. Protected by their bristles, they can live as long as 20 years.

THE PORCUPINE

The porcupine is easily recognized by its long, wiry, black-and-white bristles. The porcupine is 24 to 30 inches (60 to 76 centimeters) long, and it weighs 44 to 55 pounds (20 to 25 kilograms). The bristles are very sharp. They detach easily, and when lodged in the flesh can cause severe wounds. The feet are equipped with digging claws. The footprint is not unlike a small bear.

Porcupines are mostly seen at night. Their presence is revealed by dropped bristles which lie in their path.

Porcupines are very destructive to all root crops, bulbs and the bark of certain trees. They eat fallen fruits of all kinds. They are said to eat old bones. They remain in the hole in which they are born until the bristles have grown and hardened. Then they accompany their mother on nightly food hunts. Porcupines often travel great distances at night in search of food. I've encountered them on the road at night. They will speed up to a run with their bristles raised in alarm, causing them to look like giant pin cushions. They are cautious animals, intelligent and difficult to trap. It takes a skilled predator to attack a porcupine.

The porcupine's bristles are a defensive weapon. It will charge backward into a lion and cause the lion much damage. The bristles, when lodged in the throat, lips or jaws of a lion, cause painful swelling. This prevents the lion from hunting or eating, causing it to starve to death.

I took my assistants Robert and Mutero with me to photograph more animals. As we left camp, a hippo watched us prepare for the journey. When we crossed the river in the old makorro (muh-KOR-row) or "canoe" we had found, we came across a small herd of buffalo.

THE AFRICAN BUFFALO

We wondered if we should make a detour around them but our time was valuable and we didn't want to lose the track. We continued through the group, keeping a sharp watch on the herd. The odor of the buffalo stuck in our noses. The herd was bigger than we thought. It can be dangerous to get too near a buffalo. They are big and clumsy and the males have massive horns. They raise their heads when they get your scent. Buffalo often shake their heads in fear. If alarmed, the leader of the herd will flee, followed by the rest of the herd. A stampede would crush anyone in their path.

We had no rifles; but even if we had one it wouldn't help us much. We were thinking about retreating back to camp but we decided to press on. The bush opened into flat prairie land with low grass and heavy sand. Walking became difficult. We could not sit down to rest. What shade there was was occupied by buffalo. We were careful as we zig-zagged past the buffalo. My landmarks were trees and anthills. The hours were dragging on in the hot sun. Finally when the sun began to sink towards the horizon, it cooled down a bit. I kept thinking of hungry lions possibly following the buffalo. We had gotten off the track and didn't know if we were getting any closer to the landrover. Both my companions were terrified and I wasn't very happy myself.

Mutero pointed out a very high tree and helped me climb up to get a look. I could see a vast expanse of field and many more buffalo. Their smell was much stronger higher up than on the ground. The smell almost made me sick. In the distance I could see the Goha hills. This helped me to get my bearings straight and I knew we were walking in the right direction. Our destination was not far away. I climbed down and gave the good news to Mutero and Robert.

We moved on a few yards and found ourselves near buffalo. They were standing so close together it was hard to keep a good distance from them. The sight of their heavy horns was frightening. We were looking at many hundreds of buffalo in this herd. We had walked right into the middle of them. We tried to make ourselves small and creep through the herd like shadows.

The sun started to set, turning the sky to a red and golden glow. Darkness soon fell, making our advance very difficult. The buffalo became fewer and fewer, and finally they were gone. About 8 o'clock we were happy to reach the stranded land-rover. We made a fire and sat down to relax. Suddenly we heard a loud trampling of buffalo in the distance. We couldn't see the cloud of dust they raised, but we could smell and taste it. It was so thick, we could hardly breathe.

Buffalo usually gather in smaller groups. During the rainy season when the grass is green and the bushes and trees have green leaves you will see herds of thirty to fifty. The adult bulls have horns that are broad and stick out of the forehead like a helmet. The horns of the cows are shorter. The horns of the calves first appear as small pointed stubs.

A herd of African buffalo grazes in the lush grass after the rains. Once killed for trampling crops, they have become plentiful in the bush.

The most common cause of death among the buffalo today is malnutrition and starvation. They need a lot of room and grass to graze on.

In very old bulls the tips are almost worn away. When a herd is grazing in the long grass it creates a very peaceful impression. Very often these massive animals are accompanied by white tick-birds. The birds stand out sharply against the black bodies of the buffaloes. They pick off insects from the buffaloes' bodies. The birds look like gymnasts as they hang from the bellies of the buffaloes and move around the giant beasts. The birds also act as guards, flying high into the sky when danger approaches.

The biggest enemy of the buffalo is the lion. Sometimes young buffalo stray from the herd. You can almost be certain that lurking in the bushes is a group of lions. If it is a lone lion or a lioness, the buffalo can put up a fight. Lions will only take on buffalo if the lions are in the majority by six to one.

Buffalo have been known to gang up on a lion in an attempt to save a wounded companion. If a buffalo is badly wounded the lion can get away with his prey or wait until the herd moves before beginning to eat.

Old bulls who have been turned out by the herd are particularly vulnerable to attack by lions, but they always go down fighting. Lions are often wounded or even killed when they attack an old bull. The old bulls are easily annoyed and rather aggressive.

Buffalo bulls fight each other at mating season. The defeated animals are thrown out of the herd. Wounded buffalo are savage animals. A charging buffalo points its head forward with the horns thrown back, lowering its head sideways just as it strikes.

The base of the horns may expand to meet in the middle of the head and form a solid shield impenetrable to bullets. Buffalo drink at sunrise and after dark. They eat and rest under shade trees during the day. They also like to wallow in mud baths. In swampy country they often spend their whole time in the depths of the reed beds, swimming when necessary.

Over thirty years have passed since I saw my first giraffe. In the cool of the dusk we saw some giraffe feeding from the tree-tops, their long necks swaying from branch to branch.

THE GIRAFFE

The giraffe is one of the most beautiful animals in all creation. When a herd of giraffe is grazing in a grove of picturesque acacias trees, the sight is breathtaking. There is no doubt that people are often struck with awe and amazement by anything that is this big.

The giraffe is one of Africa's most interesting mammals. It is very tall, standing 19 feet (5.6 meters). The female is usually 2 feet (.6 meters) shorter than the male. They have very long tails, which come into good use against pesty insects.

The giraffe's coat is short and almost satiny to the touch, gleaming like a well-groomed horse. It has patches of brown over a yellowish background, with a chestnut mane. These elegant animals blend into the color of the bush. They weigh about 2,000 pounds (900 kilograms). The color pattern of their hide makes them almost unnoticeable among the trees. It is surprising how such a large animal can be overlooked until movement or a shaft of light betrays it.

Looking at the giraffe's long and flexible neck, you would think it has more vertebrae than most animals. In fact, like all mammals, it has seven vertebrae. The seven vertebrae in the giraffe's neck are longer than most mammals. A single giraffe vertebrae can measure up to 1 foot (.3 meters) in length. Their long necks bring them close to their favorite food: twigs, shoots, and new foliage found at the top of trees. Their mobile lips grab bunches of leaves or fruit. The tongue stretches out and helps to bring the food within the reach of the teeth. The giraffes tongue is very long, ribbon-shaped and well-adapted for plucking leaves from the tops of trees. The giraffe can eat leaves as high as 16 feet (4.8 meters). They can also feed on bushes and trees of only 16 to 28 inches (40 to 71 centimeters) high. The giraffe rarely grazes near the ground. It has difficulty reaching the ground with its long neck.

Acacia (uh-KAY-shuh) trees are very common in Africa. They provide a large amount of food for the giraffe. When watching the giraffe feed on thorn acacia, one is amazed to see how a hard needle-pointed thorn of about 2 inches (5 centimeters) long easily disappears between their soft lips, as if it were a tender salad.

The tongue, which may be as long as 17 inches (43 centimeters), and is very flexible. One might think that a giraffe would be unable to clean itself. There are few parts of its own body that it cannot reach with its own tongue. It also rubs itself against trees and bushes, which act like brushs. The hide is about 1 inch (2.5 centimeters) thick and very tough. Nevertheless, it is quite sensitive. It often twitches and shudders when biting flies become troublesome.

The walk of the giraffe is similar to that of a camel, with the hind leg moving in unison with the front leg on the same side.

Short horns grow out of the top of the skull. They are not true horns but bony outgrowths. The tips are covered with skin and hair, except old bulls, where the ends are worn down to bone. A giraffe's eyes are huge and veiled in long lashes, and the vision is excellent.

The walk of a giraffe is similar to that of a camel. The hind leg moves at the same time as the front leg on the same side. When galloping, the hind legs are placed well in advance of the front ones, and the giraffe moves its neck backwards and forwards in a row-boat fashion. The stride is long and sweeping. The tail twists up over the back. Like the camel, the giraffe can go without water for long periods of time. Other animals might die from thirst while the giraffe survives in comfort on the sap contained in the leaves that it eats. It is very difficult for the giraffe to lower itself to drink from water pools. It involves a series of jerky lowerings, with the front legs straddled farther and farther apart. Despite the apparent clumsiness of this position, a giraffe can stand straight up with surprising swiftness when startled while drinking.

Because the giraffe's neck is so long, the animal needs an extremely high blood pressure so that the blood may reach the towering head. But what happens when the giraffe lowers its head more than 6 feet (1.8 meters) below the heart's level to take a drink? Scientists who have studied the giraffe's head and blood system have found that this living skyscraper is designed to cope with the problem. Nature has equipped the giraffe with an automatic valve to control the blood supply. With this valve there is neither brain hemorrhage upon lowering the head, or sudden draining of the blood when the head is quickly raised.

Let's take a look at the giraffe coming to the waterhole to drink. It appears in the clearing from the bushes. It pauses and surveys the scene carefully from under its long eyelashes. A bird is sitting between the two skin-covered horns, clearing the animals coat of insects. It is about 1640 feet (500 meters) from the bush to the waterhole. The giraffe approaches with great caution. It stops frequently to look around and takes only a few steps at a time. With its height advantage of 18 feet (5.5 meters), it should have a good view of the area. So why does it hesitate? It has great eyesight, recognizing its companions over a distance of more than a 1 mile (1.6 km). Its progress from the bush to the water can take up to two hours.

Having arrived at the water, it checks the surroundings again before starting to drink. Then it begins the process of getting down to the water. First the left foreleg is extended a little, then the right, and so on from side to side until the head is within reach of the water. The eyes are raised all the time, watching out for danger. Once down, it drinks for quite a while. Suddenly, a jump and the giraffe stands up on all fours. What was the reason for this sudden reaction? Maybe the movement of a crocodile in the water? The tall animal turns around quickly and runs away, giving the appearance that it is gliding or sailing without any movement at all. It vanishes back into the bush. Galloping giraffes have been clocked at up to 30 miles/hr. (48 k/hr.).

It is said that giraffes are totally mute, but this is not quite true. They do grunt from time to time, and if frightened they snort loudly. They live in small family groups, rising to thirty in number at times. The males are taller and have darker coloring. Individual giraffes come and go, joining this group and that. It is probably because the animals can see and recognize each other so well there is no need for the herding instinct.

Its awkward posture renders the giraffe vulnerable to predators while drinking. One or two are always on the alert, waiting until another keeps watch before they drink.

The giraffes' height allows it to get to food sources which are inaccessible to other animals.

The baby giraffe looks very out of proportion, with its huge shoulders and knees, short neck and large head. Shortly after its birth, the baby giraffe will stand on its wobbly legs seeking nourishment from its mother.

Giraffes are very gentle animals and have never been known to kill each other. The male giraffes can be seen fighting, swinging their heavy heads like clubs from side to side. Giraffes are always accompanied by large numbers of tick birds.

The tall animals will often lie down to rest, but they usually keep their head erect. A better way to doze is to stay on their feet and to hook their head into a fork in a tree.

The only means of defense for a giraffe is kicking. Their chief enemy is the lion, with leopards launching attacks on the young giraffes. The giraffe often gallops through thick brush when being chased by a lion. With its strong hide it can stand the scratches from the bushes. The lion will always fall back out of the brush. Giraffes are seldom bothered by any form of animal. But sometimes they are attacked by crocodiles when they are drinking water. Despite their huge size and ability to kick, giraffes are not mean. They seem content to live in peace with all the other animals of the African plains. Zebra, ostriches and impala are often seen in or near their company. It is their ability to spot danger from far off which gives the other animals a certain feeling of security. Before running away the giraffe will move its tail from side to side, giving an alarm signal to all others in the area.

The elephant is, of course, much heavier than the giraffe. An elephant can weigh six tons (5443 kg.) against the 2866 pounds (1300 kilograms) of a big giraffe. The shoulder height of both animals might even be the same, but the giraffe carries its head high above and can actually look down its nose at the mighty elephant.

The family of Cercopithecide (ser-co-PITH-i-side) includes monkeys and baboons. Those best known and commonly seen in Botswana are the vervet monkey and the baboon.

THE VERVET MONKEY

Vervet monkeys are lightly built with small round heads and grey coats intermingled with yellow. They have naked black faces with white side-whiskers and their tales are extremely long, up to 30 inches (76 centimeters). The body length is 20 to 24 inches (50 to 60 centimeters). They have dainty hands and feet with thumbs and perfectly shaped flat nails almost like a human being. A large male weighs about 5 pounds (2.5 kg). They are excellent mimics.

Vervets associate in troops of 20 to 30, living in forest or bush country. They are usually found very close to water. Their diet includes berries, bulbs, seeds, wild fruits, resin from certain trees, young birds and insects. During the day they are found on the ground looking for food. At night they roost high in the treetops.

The intelligence of the vervet monkey cannot be compared with that of the baboon. What the baboon lacks in beauty it makes up in intelligence. Campfire tales say that baboons have been trained to be shepherds. A tame baboon is easily angered. It becomes stubborn if it is mocked or teased. The baboon is big, powerful, and ape-like. It has bushy eyebrows, a snout like a dog, long sharp teeth, long legs, and a long tail reaching 24 inches (60 centimeters). The male weighs up to 100 pounds (45 kilograms), the female half as much.

Vervet monkeys are lightly built with small round heads. They have delicate hands and feet with thumbs and nails almost like a human being.

The baboon lives in rocky country and thick brush. It sleeps in the fork of a tree. It likes the more rugged parts of the terrain which man cannot reach. It is found in areas where the plains animals have long been driven away.

THE BABOON

Baboons are amazing rock climbers. The most hard-to-reach spots on a cliff are their shelters. They owe their survival to this unusual skill. The baboon has no friends. The hills are its last refuge. Here it picks up a meager living, turning over stones to get at scorpions and millipedes. It scrapes roots and bulbs from the soil. The baboon will eat what is available. No birds nest is safe from them, no matter how high it may be in the rocks. They also like to move about on the ground. They forage for food in parties in a spread-out formation.

Baboons are a menace to any cropland. The natives build shelters around their crops to protect them from the baboon raids. The natives have to watch for baboons day and night if they want to have a harvest. Baboons sleep at night huddled in caves. They begin to hunt at dawn. In recent years, baboons have been known to kill sheep because of the lack of food. With their huge teeth they can tear apart their prey in a matter of seconds. Not even a fierce killer leopard will face an angry group of baboons.

The females, when quietly foraging, carry their young on their backs. When in a hurry or climbing, they sling them under their breast and let them hold onto their fur with all four limbs.

Baboons are a menace to every farmer's crops. In recent years, baboons have been known to kill sheep, probably because of the lack of food.

Young baboons are full of fun. They play and slide in the sand with great enjoyment. But the older baboons become mean and ill-tempered. There is an unusual community spirit and they become very attached to their young.

If a companion is in trouble, all the baboons run to help with their combined strength. Confronted with their sharp claws and powerful jaws, the enemy often flees. Baboons see and hear very well, but the sense of smell is not much better than that of an average human being. With their keen eyesight they are often placed in charge of the general animal communitys lookout position. The baboon is quick to attack if frightened.

Their biggest enemy is the leopard. Lions are also their enemies. When angered or frightened the baboon is very noisy. Barking and screaming goes on for hours if one of them is killed. Normally they just chatter to one another in a relaxed fashion. A interesting feature about baboons is their talent for observation. They usually stay clear of men but behave as they like in the presence of less aggressive womenkind. Their behavior depends on whether the human being is wearing a skirt or pants. Women in slacks also command their respect.

Once I saw a lion kill a baboon at a waterhole. The other baboons fled and took refuge in a tree without leaves. There were no other trees nearby so they couldn't continue their escape without coming down. They stayed there making loud noises and barking for three hours until the lions went away.

On another occasion, we were all in camp at night with a bright fire burning to keep the predators away. Suddenly the baboons started making a loud noise.

Shortly afterwards we could hear something crashing through the brush nearby. A buck broke through chased by a lion. The lion killed the buck near our tent. It then settled down to feed and we could hear the tearing, crunching and growling. The single lion was joined by two others. We all drew nearer to the fire. We stayed up late until the lions finished their meal. After the kill, a dead silence had fallen. There were no night noises at all. Even the baboons remained silent.

I once saw baboons chasing a leopard. It was on a rocky hill-top with lots of bush. They kept going around and around in the same circle, the leopard first, then about 18 baboons in hot pursuit, barking and running fast. Eventually on one of the circles only the baboons emerged from the bush; there was no leopard. It might have hidden in the bush and grabbed the last baboon to follow. There was one baboon missing from the group. I waited an hour and then the leopard emerged carry-ing a portion of its kill. The other baboons had given up and run off long before.

Breakfast was called for 6 a.m., when everyone was rather tired. We made off in silence to hunt the leopard with the camera. Mutero, who had been out early in the morning, had spotted a large herd of buffalo from a hilltop. We walked towards the hill, passing an impala surrounded by grunting warthogs. Then we saw something with horns lying in the grass, which looked like an impala. As we got nearer, some warthogs stared at us with their small eyes, tense and suspicious. They held their positions until we were about 10 foot (3 meters) from them. They finally made off with their tails in the air. We found a buck, dead but still warm, with a slash on its neck. Mutero's sharp eyes spotted a leopard in the bush 33 feet (10 meters) away.

Then we saw another leopard slinking off. We retreated cautiously. After a few paces backwards we found an anthill, ideally situated to act as cover, and there we waited with the camera. The area was ideal for leopard. There was a waterhole nearby, which by day was crowded with baboons. They were present then, making a good deal of noise. On the edge of the waterhole was a small hill with big trees leaning out over the water. From these trees the leopard could easily choose its next meal.

Our leopard didn't move at all. Peter asked how long we intended to sit there. It was very quiet. Even the baboons had quieted down. It was very hot, about 90 degrees Fahrenheit (30 degrees Centigrade). We made a shelter with green branches to get some shade. I said: "We'll stay until we have the leopards on film."

THE LEOPARD

The leopard is probably the wildest animal in Africa. The male measures up to 6 feet (1.8 meters) from nose to tail. Its shoulder height is 30 inches (76 centimeters). It is not very heavy, weighing between 110 and 176 pounds (50 and 80 kilograms). The female is 22 pounds (10 kilograms) lighter. The body is long and slender with short strong legs. They have black spots with the darkest in the middle of the body, and white whiskers with cold, pale, greenish-yellow eyes. As in all members of the cat family, the jaws are very strong. The claws are retractable. The young leopards have long soft fur. Leopards live in rocky country and forest areas. Their markings provide them with excellent camouflage.

More powerful than the cheetah, the leopard can kill larger prey such as wildebeest. However, it is the main predator of baboons, especially at night.

Judging by the number of fresh tracks found early in the day, leopards seem to be active mostly at night. But if the leopard is undisturbed it will hunt at any hour of the day. It likes to lie up in rocks or in the tops of trees. It is said that leopards spend half their lifetime lying in trees.

Leopards are very good climbers. They use their long sharp claws to dig into the bark and pull themselves up the straightest tree. A leopard often makes its kill from a tree, pouncing from above onto the prey below. This includes antelope like impala, bushbuck, kudu and tsessebe. To protect their young from leopards, some antelope hide their calves for the first few weeks of life. The leopards favorite food is monkeys and baboons. Any pack of wild dogs can scare a leopard away. A leopard will never take on more than one dog.

Monkeys and leopards maintain a constant feud. Leopards on the ground make monkeys very angry and nervous. Monkeys follow the leopards from the treetops with loud cries and warnings. The leopard has learned to turn this to its advantage. They hunt in pairs. While one strolls along the ground engaging the monkeys' attention, its partner waits to attack the ones in the treetops. Baboons are also hunted in this fashion. But baboons are fierce and have strong community spirit. When a leopard catches one it runs off at top speed rather than face being torn limb-from-limb by a mad baboon.

The leopard attacks its prey first on the back of the neck, and strikes an artery with its front paw. It then tears out the throat before going on to eat the flesh. A leopard can feed on the same victim for three to four days. Although a leopard might make a kill during the day, most of their eating is done at night.

What they cannot eat, they store. Leopards will hoist their victims high into a tree away from the other predators such as the lion, cheetah, hyena and wild dogs. They have been known to carry a weight of 154 pounds (70 kilograms) up a branchless tree, proof of their agility and power.

The leopard is a vocal animal. It makes a sound similar to coughing or sawing wood. In areas not disturbed by humans, it reveals its presence by a rasping grunt. After each grunt it breathes deeply with a snoring noise. An angry leopard growls almost like a lion. It is believed that the coughing is part of its territorial call.

There are many animals in the bush country of Africa, each with its own unique traits. We shall continue our search of new species perhaps not yet seen by man.

GLOSSARY

Acacia Tree - a tree from which gum is obtained.

Africa - a continent (large body of land) south of the Mediterranean Sea between the Atlantic and Indian Ocean.

Anthill - a dirt mound over an ant's nest.

Baboon - a large African monkey.

Botswana - a country in southeastern Africa.

Buffalo - a kind of ox found in Asia and southern Africa.

Bush - wild, remote, uncultivated land.

Cheetah - a kind of leopard. Of the cat family, found in Africa.

Crocodile - a large reptile with thick skin, a long tail, and huge jaws.

Expedition - a journey for a particular purpose.

Giraffe - a long-necked African animal, yellowish in color.

Hippopotamus - a large African river animal with tusks, short legs, and thick skin.

Impala - a small antelope of southern Africa.

Kudu - a type of antelope found in Africa.

Leopard - a large African and Asian flesh-eating animal of the cat family.

Makorro - a canoe made of wood by the African Bushmen.

Mammal - a member of the class of animals that raise their young on mothers milk.

Ostrich - a swift-running African bird that cannot fly which buries its head in the sand.

Plain - a large area of level ground.

Porcupine - a rodent with a body and a tail covered by protective bristles.

Predator - an animal that preys upon others.

Prey - an animal that is hunted or killed by another for food.

Scientist - an expert in one or more of the natural or physical sciences.

Scorpion - a small animal of the spider group with lobster-like claws and a stinger in its tail.

Terrain - a stretch of land, with regard to its natural features.

Tick Birds - birds that eat insects off animals.

Tsessebe - a type of antelope found in Africa.

Tusk - one of a pair of long pointed teeth that project outside the mouth in certain animals.

Vertebrae - any of the bones or segments that form the backbone.

Vervet Monkey - a small African monkey.

Warthog - a kind of African pig with two large tusks and warts on its face.

INDEX: